Make Peace *with* Your Past

Living a Life with No Regrets

GREGORY L. JANTZ, PHD
WITH KEITH WALL

Make Peace with Your Past: Living a Life with No Regrets

Published by Aspire Press,
an imprint of Tyndale House Ministries,
Carol Stream, Illinois
rose-publishing.com

ISBN: 978-1-4964-8123-8

The views and opinions expressed in this book are those of the author(s) and do not necessarily express the views of Tyndale House Ministries or Aspire Press, nor is this book intended to be a substitute for mental health treatment or professional counseling. The information in this resource is intended as a guideline for healthy living. Please consult qualified medical, legal, pastoral, and psychological professionals regarding individual concerns.

Tyndale House Ministries and Aspire Press are in no way liable for any content, change of content, or activity for the works listed. Citation of a work does not mean endorsement of all its contents or of other works by the same author.

Printed in the United States of America
31 30 29 28 27 26 25
7 6 5 4 3 2 1

Contents

INTRODUCTION

It's Time *to* Make Peace *with* Your Past

Here is a product label you'll probably never see: "SURGEON GENERAL'S WARNING: Living in the past is hazardous to your health."

Yet many people show unmistakable symptoms of "time sickness." Like oxygen-deprived mountain climbers who lose their mental grip, they stagger and stumble aimlessly, stuck in the past and unable to live freely in the present.

They struggle to overcome anxiety, depression, and regret, because their mind continually travels back to mistakes they made, traumas they endured, and hurts they caused.

Unfortunately, they often miss the joys and delights right before them every day.

Everybody wants to feel energized, optimistic, and fulfilled. We want to wake up each morning eagerly looking forward to the day ahead, rather than dreading it.

WARNING: LIVING IN THE PAST IS HAZARDOUS TO YOUR HEALTH.

We want to enjoy our work, relationships, and hobbies, thankful for the meaningful people and activities that fill our lives.

We want to go to bed at night knowing we will sleep peacefully and deeply, feeling content and satisfied.

We want to feel alive, not numb.

We want to feel hopeful, not hopeless.

We want to feel grateful, not bitter.

If you haven't experienced living with this kind of joy and vitality, it's quite possible you have not made peace with your past.

Are you carrying the deep pain of past regrets? Are you angry with yourself for making mistakes that had far-reaching consequences? Do you lie awake at night wondering how your life could have been different if you had not made foolish choices that harmed yourself or others? You are not alone.

Or perhaps the pain of your past was not your own doing. Maybe you have suffered from the bad choices and mistakes of others. Do you view yourself in the shameful way that toxic people from your past did? It's all too easy to listen to people who implied or said outright, "You don't measure up. You're no good. You'll never amount to much."

The reality for most of us, however, is that we have experienced a combination of personal regrets and mistreatment from others. To add insult to injury, the pain we suffer at the hands of others often contributes in some way to our own bad choices.

People weighed down and held back by the past often feel they are in a captivity of sorts—trapped and immobilized by a force bigger than themselves. When you are struggling with depression or anxiety about your past, it's difficult to feel enthused about the future—if you can envision one at all.

Does this describe how you're feeling? If so, I have fantastic news: It doesn't have to be this way! You can have clarity and peace about where you've been

WHATEVER IS BEHIND THE PAIN OF YOUR PAST, GOD OFFERS FREEDOM.

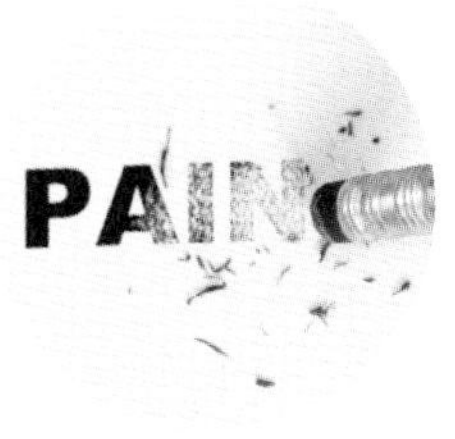

and where you're going. Your hurts can be soothed and your burdens relieved.

Are you ready to renew your dreams and refresh your energy to achieve them? Whatever is behind the pain of your past, God offers freedom. He is powerful enough to help you deal with the consequences of your past and steer your life in a better direction.

Allow the principles and practical steps in this book to equip you to look back on your past in a way that brings fresh perspective to your present and optimistic hope for your future. You'll explore several keys for moving beyond regrets, failures, and the pain of hurts and heartaches. As you do so, I encourage you to reflect on the following life-changing words from the book of Jeremiah:

> *"I know the plans I have for you," declares the* Lord, *"plans to prosper you and not to harm you, plans to give you hope and a future. Then you will call on me and come and pray to me, and I will listen to you. You will seek me and find me*

> *when you seek me with all your heart. I will be found by you," declares the* Lord, *"and will bring you back from captivity."*
>
> Jeremiah 29:11–14

Embrace these words as you pursue your own emotional, spiritual, and physical wellness. They offer hope that although your past may have been disappointing or even disastrous, your present and your future can be better than you ever imagined. You *can* make peace with your past.

CHAPTER 1

Move *from* Hurting *to* Healing

As a twenty-year-old college sophomore returning home for Thanksgiving break in 2009, Mary "Mo" Isom found herself hanging upside down by her seat belt at 1:30 a.m., trapped alone inside her wrecked car and struggling to breathe.

Mo had lost control of her Jeep, hit an embankment, flipped over three times, and landed upside down in a ditch. The accident resulted in terrible injuries for Mo, including a broken neck, fractured ribs, serious bruises on her brain, and injuries to her lungs and liver.

Even as Mo choked on her own blood and writhed in pain, God's presence flooded her vehicle. His voice spoke strongly to her heart. Despite her life-threatening situation, the first words out of Mo's mouth were not curses or painful moans. Instead, Mo kept saying, "God is beautiful. God is beautiful. God is beautiful." [1]

This was quite curious to the man who had been driving the same stretch of road when he saw Mo's lights flicker and swerve. A retired paramedic and a Navyman, he stopped to investigate and spotted Mo's twisted Jeep in the ditch. Expecting to find a dead body, the man made his way toward the wreckage. By then Mo had somehow slipped out of her seat belt, and he found her lying on the ceiling of the Jeep's interior.

"God is beautiful. God is beautiful. God is beautiful," Mo repeated with a smile on her face.

"That's great," the retired paramedic said as he tried to gently remove her from the mangled vehicle, "but if we can just get you out ..."

As Mo's life hung in the balance, she was forever changed. It was the moment she came to understand that she was loved and forgiven—the moment she started the journey from hurting to healing—toward the freedom of making peace with her past.

Spiraling Downward

Mo grew up in a close-knit family that included her parents, John and Heidi, and her older sister, Sloan.

They faithfully attended a local church, and Mo's father was a well-known attorney. In high school, six-foot Mo excelled on the soccer field and became one of the nation's top goalkeepers.

AS MO'S LIFE HUNG IN THE BALANCE, SHE WAS FOREVER CHANGED.

But underneath this ideal exterior, trouble brewed on several fronts. Mo's dad pushed her hard in her budding soccer career. When she played well, he was affirming and complimentary. When she didn't, he often gave her the silent treatment.

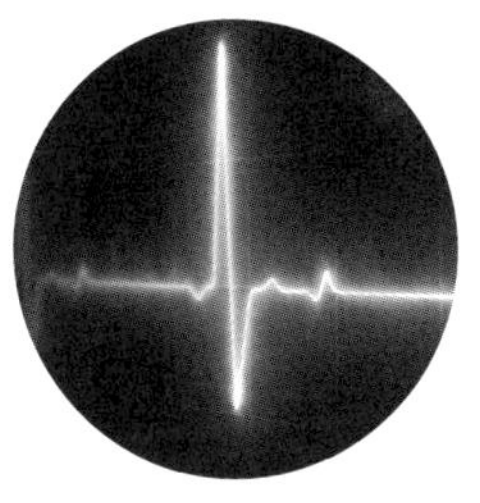

The social pressures to look beautiful and be accepted by the popular crowd also weighed heavily on Mo. Feeling she didn't always measure up, Mo developed an image crisis. As so many teens do, she hid her insecurities by putting up a front of faked perfection. But the more she tried to control her life by achieving success at school, on the soccer field, and in beauty pageants, the more she lost control of her life.

Eventually, Mo fell victim to an eating disorder. For three and a half years, she hid her problem until she was desperate enough to pray for help and confess her struggle to her mom. Working with a counselor and a nutritionist, Mo eventually found healing and set her sights on the next challenge: her freshman year at Louisiana State University. Ranking as one of the top six senior goalkeepers in the nation, Mo had earned a full-ride scholarship to LSU.

Meanwhile, however, Mo's dad had been dealing with his own serious struggles, including unpaid taxes and the use of pornography. Still, John tried to be a dedicated father and husband. Like clockwork, he always arrived home by 5:30 p.m. on weeknights. That's why it was strange when he didn't come home the evening of January 2, 2009, when Mo was home on Christmas break.

THE MORE MO TRIED TO CONTROL HER LIFE, THE MORE SHE LOST CONTROL OF HER LIFE.

John had left a voice mail for Heidi, saying he just needed to drive around and clear his head. There was also a note by the phone: "I do love you." Early in the morning on January 3, Heidi discovered a four-paragraph suicide note that John had emailed to her. Mo woke up to her mother screaming, "Get in the car! Get in the car! Grab your shoes; grab your things! Get in the car!" After a frantic but fruitless search around town, Heidi, Mo, and Sloan learned the horrific news from local police: John had died of a self-inflicted gunshot wound in a hotel room located several hours away in a different state.

Mo went into an emotional tailspin. To retain some sense of normalcy, she returned a few weeks later to Louisiana State. She put on a mask and tried to act like everything was fine, numbing her pain by partying, drinking too much alcohol, and pushing sexual boundaries. But the more she did those things, the emptier she felt.

Mo was in so much emotional pain that she briefly considered taking the same path her father had chosen. In her anger and anguish, she cried out in prayer, "God, if you're so real, just wreck my life, because I'm just tired of living it. And if you're so real, reveal yourself in some way that I just can't miss it."

> "BE STILL, AND KNOW THAT I AM GOD."
>
> —PSALM 46:10

In fact, that's exactly what God did when her Jeep spun out of control during that fateful trip home the following November. When Mo regained consciousness as she hung upside down, the presence of God was strong. The words of Psalm 46:10 came to her: "Be still, and know that I am God."

Despite her near-death experience, Mo felt overwhelming peace. Before long, the retired paramedic arrived and pulled her from the mashed heap of metal. The wreck was a wake-up call for Mo—the beginning of her journey of moving from hurting to healing. In the months that followed, Mo started putting the physical, emotional, mental, and spiritual pieces of her life back together as she made peace with her past.

"That wreck was brutal, and the injuries were brutal," she says. "But I was brought from death to life in that car. My soul was saved in that place."

Starting Your Journey

For some of us, the journey from hurting or regret to healing and hope involves a dramatic series of events like Mo experienced. For others, the transition is a prolonged journey, with small steps forward over time. Whatever the cause of your pain, you can still make peace with your past and, in the process, gain a deeper understanding of yourself and life. Here are four principles to help you get started.

1 Keep a Balanced Perspective

Everyone on planet Earth has endured life's hurts and heartaches, and everyone has their own set of mistakes and list of ways they have hurt others. Some are terribly severe and others less so. But all are real and not to be dismissed.

Chances are, the longer you've lived, the more regrets you've piled up and the more emotional scars you have to show. Broken relationships, financial calamity, and the death of a loved one are just a few examples of hurts that people can inflict on others or experience themselves. Such is the reality of fallen people living in a fallen world.

"I WAS BROUGHT FROM DEATH TO LIFE IN THAT CAR."
—MO ISOM

When you least expect it, memories of foolish actions from the past can invade your thoughts and destroy your peace. Those regrettable events have the potential to loom larger than life and overwhelm you with the message that you're a total failure.

Yet the truth of the matter is that you are not alone in your mistakes and shame. Every person on earth is vulnerable to missteps, and whether an offense is minor or horrific, the fact remains that we are all created by God with a unique and loving purpose—yourself included.

As you move from hurting to healing, it's important to keep this balanced perspective in mind.

2 Choose Who Will Define Your Worth

Validation is the recognition and acceptance of another person's thoughts, feelings, sensations, and behaviors as understandable. *Self-validation* is the recognition and acceptance of your own thoughts, feelings, sensations, and behaviors as understandable. It's a way of honoring who you are, what you feel, and what you believe.

WHATEVER THE CAUSE OF YOUR PAIN, YOU CAN STILL MAKE PEACE WITH YOUR PAST.

People who lack validation in their lives fail to understand their own intrinsic value. Without this, a person will often look to the passing whims of circumstances and culture to provide a framework for their worth.

It is easy to fall into the trap of thinking your worth as a person comes from what you do instead of who you are. It's also easy to perceive your worth as a reflection of what others think instead of allowing it to shine out from your own confident assurance. And when you allow other people or outside situations to define your worth, you make yourself a hostage to them.

Despite the ways you have disappointed yourself, you are a person with great potential. Despite the regrets or hurts you carry from the past, the fact is that you are a person of infinite worth.

> "I PRAISE YOU BECAUSE I AM FEARFULLY AND WONDERFULLY MADE."
>
> —PSALM 139:14

Notice I didn't say you create or cause your own worth. Each of us has a value that we did not generate. This value is a gift from God. He made you who you are and loves you for who you are.

This is the bedrock foundation for self-worth anchored in God; this is your special identity, safe and protected in God's hands. As you move from hurting to healing, remember that God created you for a purpose, and that purpose is good.

3 Learn from Your Past

The hard truth is that you will learn far more from pain and loss than you will from a life of success or void of challenges. The crucible of suffering is an outstanding instructor—if you allow it to be. An essential element of moving from hurting to healing is being open to the life lessons that painful experiences teach and the character they build.

Research backs this up as well. According to one study, "people with a history of *some* lifetime adversity reported better mental health and well-being outcomes than not only people with a *high* history of adversity but also than people with *no* history of adversity"[2] (emphasis added). Time-honored wisdom from the Bible confirms the value of hardship:

YOU WILL LEARN FAR MORE FROM PAIN AND LOSS THAN YOU WILL FROM A LIFE OF SUCCESS OR VOID OF CHALLENGES.

> *We can rejoice, too, when we run into problems and trials, for we know that they help us develop endurance. And endurance develops strength of character, and character strengthens our confident hope of salvation. And this hope will not lead to disappointment. For we know how dearly God loves us.*
>
> Romans 5:3–5 nlt

EIGHT WAYS TO GLEAN WISDOM FROM YOUR PAST

You've heard the axiom, "Those who do not learn from history are bound to repeat it." Some people experience ongoing difficulties because they've never taken a hard look at the past to see how it affects their present and future.

But let's emphasize the positive: Everyone can gain valuable insights by exploring their personal history. Gleaning wisdom from your past will improve your life in every way. Here's how to get started.

1. **Consider how your family of origin shaped you.** All of us are largely products of the families we grew up in. We are shaped and molded in thousands of ways by our parents and extended family members. How is this true for you?
2. **Identify the turning points in your life.** Everyone has experienced significant events (some positive, some painful) that redirect or reshape their lives. What were yours?
3. **Weigh the words of wisdom that stuck with you.** Perhaps a parent, teacher, or coach gave you some advice—or lived in a way that served as advice. How did that affect who you are today?

4. **Unpack your life in five-year increments.** In a notebook or journal, write out the main events from each five-year segment of your life.

5. **Gauge how you have changed over the past ten or twenty years.** Everyone grows and develops as time passes. In what ways are you different from the person you were a decade or two ago?

6. **Assess your successes.** What do you consider your most successful events and experiences? What qualities did you bring to these achievements?

7. **Examine your failures.** Psychologists often say we learn most from our failures. Mine them for all they're worth.

8. **Notice how your dreams have changed.** The dreams you have now likely aren't the same ones you had in the past. What circumstances or lessons led them to change? After reflecting more on your past, do you find your dreams are shifting yet again?

4 Talk It Out

If your interpretations of the past or expectations for the future are off track, you may need help dividing the facts from the fiction you've bought into.

As you might suspect, I am a big believer in engaging in therapy with a skilled, experienced practitioner who can help you identify the thought patterns that are keeping you mired in pain.

Whether with a therapist, a spiritual mentor, or a trusted friend, putting your feelings into words will help you take steps toward inner peace and bolster your emotional health in many ways.

THE PATH OF LIFE WAS NEVER MEANT TO BE WALKED ALONE.

I agree with psychologist Georgia Witkin, who describes talking as "one of our natural, built-in, therapeutic capacities. We use our words to express what we want and need, and the same should be for our feelings."[3]

Psychology professor and author Steven C. Hayes also notes, "There is a myth in Western countries about the so-called 'self-made person,' and how we all should strive to become, well, self-made. But nobody is an island, and we all need other people."[4]

WHY TALK IT OUT?

- Hearing our internal thoughts expressed externally can actually reveal the path forward.
- It's an active step toward a solution, even if the solution isn't immediately evident.
- It gives us a chance to hear the helpful perspectives of others.

Mo Isom subscribes to this principle of talking it out. She experienced healing when she started sharing her story. "In this fake-it-till-you-make-it culture," she said, "it's amazing to see when you do just show those vulnerabilities ... when you don't worry anymore about this faked perfection, but you just bear the dirty laundry, how much community it creates in people saying, 'I went through the same thing.'"

It's true. Everyone goes through hard times, and faithful friends will shine the brightest in those moments. They might not be able to fix your problem, but their love, support, and encouragement can make a huge difference.

The path of life was never meant to be walked alone. Proverbs 17:17 says, "A friend loves at all times." Your real friends will rise to the occasion when you need them most, so talk to them. Share with them. Lean on them. Chances are, you'll be able to return the favor one day.

■ ■ ■

Today, Mo Isom is a completely different person from the one who pleaded with God to wreck her life. A few weeks after her car accident, she began sharing her story online and attracted many people who could relate to her pain. Since then, Mo finished her undergraduate degree, got married, became a mom, published books, and started a ministry called Boldlife Initiative. Over the past several years, she has spoken at hundreds of conferences, schools, and churches.

REAL FRIENDS RISE TO THE OCCASION WHEN YOU NEED THEM MOST.

"Injuries heal, and you can buy a new car, but we have moments in our life where we have the freedom to choose whom we will serve, and that choice can change everything," she said.

It wasn't always easy—her life literally had to be flipped upside down. But because she chose to persist in moving from hurting to healing, she is in a far better spot today than she was in that wrecked Jeep in 2009.

That's Mo's making-peace-with-her-past story. What will yours be? In the next chapter, we'll take a look at an important step in writing that story.

CHAPTER 2

Forgive Those Who Hurt You

Gina could hear the frustration in her sister's voice, mixed with a heavy dose of anger and resentment.

"I don't understand how you can stand to be around her!" Patricia sneered. "How can you forget what she was like when we were growing up?"

"I haven't forgotten what she was like," Gina replied. "I've *forgiven* her for what she was like."

It wasn't the first time Gina and her sister had replayed this conversation. In fact, they seemed to have the same intense discussion each Christmas—the one day a year Patricia could muster the courage and fortitude to be around her mother.

Two years apart in age, Gina and Patricia were now in their early thirties. They had survived childhood by protecting and comforting each other amid their mother's constant criticism, relentless put-downs, and frequent episodes of rage.

She had been a single parent since the girls were young, when their father died suddenly at age forty-one of a brain aneurysm. Angry that her husband had "left her" to raise the girls on her own, with little money and no help from extended family, Gina and Patricia's mom took the loss hard and seemed to view it as a personal affront.

Her burning anger, often fueled by too much booze, was directed toward Gina and Patricia, the scapegoats for her miserable life. They had endured years of withering scorn and emotional abuse before graduating from high school and moving out of the house. How the two dealt with such a painful upbringing is a study in stark contrasts.

Gina had gone through the process of releasing the pain of the past. She now made a point to spend time with their mother regularly. Patricia, on the other hand, still held on tightly to her painful and shame-filled memories, refusing to engage in anything more than the obligatory annual Christmas visit. She couldn't stand to be around her mother for longer than was absolutely necessary, and she didn't understand how Gina could.

"Even if I could let go of the past, she's still the same old Mom—negative, judgmental, and critical. She drives me nuts!" Patricia said.

HOW GINA AND PATRICIA DEALT WITH A PAINFUL UPBRINGING IS A STUDY IN STARK CONTRASTS.

Gina paused a moment, giving careful thought to her response.

"Once I forgave her," she said, "it took away a lot of her power to drive me nuts. I'm not mad at her anymore over the past, so when she starts into that behavior now, I'm able to set boundaries and shield myself."

"How could you forgive someone who hasn't even asked for it?" Patricia asked, as she had so many times before. "She damaged us badly, and she's never taken responsibility for any of her terrible behavior."

"I could forgive her because it's my decision, not hers," replied Gina. "I needed to forgive her more than she wanted to be forgiven. I did it for my sake as much as for her sake. I just didn't want to live with all that anger and bitterness anymore. The only way to let it go was to forgive."

Navigating *the* Path *of* Forgiveness

There is a proven antidote for toxic emotions and the inability to make peace with your past—and it's also a powerful tonic for regaining control over your health and well-being.

Proof lies in the millions of people who have gone before you and found freedom in the age-old practice of *forgiveness*.

As Gina and Patricia discovered, some painful life experiences cannot be mitigated, fixed, or erased. They can only be forgiven.

Making peace with your past begins when you choose to forgive those who have hurt you. Take the following principles to heart as you start your journey.

1 Know the Dangers of Unforgiveness

I am well aware that *forgiveness* is a loaded word for many people. To some, it carries forced religious overtones or hints of pop-culture sentimentalism they have learned to mistrust. Often when I touch on the topic of forgiveness with clients who are struggling to work through broken or embittered relationships from the past, they are incredulous.

Yet experience has proven that hanging on to offenses and emotional wounds is an effective (and unfortunate) way to punish *yourself*. As the old adage goes, "Before you embark on a journey of revenge, dig two graves." Chronic anger from unforgiveness can negatively affect your "heart rate, blood pressure, and immune response," which in turn can lead to "depression, heart disease and diabetes, and other conditions."[5]

"THE ONLY WAY TO LET IT GO WAS TO FORGIVE."
—GINA

2 Embrace the Blessings of Forgiveness

God's loving desire is that we avoid the dangers of unforgiveness and reap the benefits that forgiveness brings. Here are just two examples where his Word highlights this sentiment:

> *Do not judge, and you will not be judged. Do not condemn, and you will not be condemned. Forgive, and you will be forgiven.*
>
> LUKE 6:37

Get rid of all bitterness, rage and anger, brawling and slander, along with every form of malice. Be kind and compassionate to one another, forgiving each other, just as in Christ God forgave you.

EPHESIANS 4:31–32

MAKING PEACE WITH YOUR PAST BEGINS WHEN YOU CHOOSE TO FORGIVE THOSE WHO HAVE HURT YOU.

As we forgive, we begin to put behind us the regrets and offenses that have defined us. Extending forgiveness is key to the peace we're looking for when dealing with our past. Initially it's difficult to imagine forgiving ourselves for that awful deed or forgiving someone else who deeply hurt us. It's contrary to our very nature and opposes our strong desire for justice.

Yet make no mistake, forgiving ourselves and our perpetrators—whether they're sorry or not—is incredibly beneficial for our own sense of inner peace and our physical, mental, and spiritual well-being. According to the Mayo Clinic, the blessings of forgiveness can include:

- Healthier relationships
- Improved mental health
- Less anxiety, stress, and hostility
- Fewer symptoms of depression
- Lower blood pressure
- A stronger immune system
- Improved heart health
- Improved self-esteem[6]

3 Understand What Forgiveness *Isn't*

Because there is so much confusion about forgiveness, it's important for us to dig a little deeper. Let's shine the light of truth on a few misconceptions about forgiveness that keep people stuck in bondage to their angry and fearful judgments toward those who have wronged them.

It Doesn't Excuse the Action

The sticking point for most people is a burning desire for justice. They can't bear to let someone "get away with" perpetrating a hurtful offense. But ignoring or overlooking someone's misdeeds is not the essence of forgiveness at all. Rather, it's about whether you want to go on reliving the pain of life's inevitable conflicts—or let go and move on.

The misunderstanding lies in the belief that forgiving someone is the same as excusing the offense. But the truth is that when we forgive, the offender is still responsible for what they have done. Forgiveness is not primarily about giving something to the one who caused us harm, but about giving *ourselves* permission to release the toxic grip of our past.

HANGING ON TO OFFENSES AND EMOTIONAL WOUNDS IS AN EFFECTIVE (AND UNFORTUNATE) WAY TO PUNISH *YOURSELF*.

When we hang on to feelings of injustice and the desire for payback, we keep the offense alive and the wounds fresh. And in the process, the negative physical and psychological effects of anger and fear continue to eat away at us.

The choice is yours: Will you cling to the offense and its effects, making matters worse for yourself? Or will you let go of the need for "justice" and answers to vague and fruitless questions like "Why me?"

Forgiving the one who hurt you is the key to escaping this trap. You don't need to excuse his or her actions or protect them from any fallout, but you *can* determine in your heart to no longer hold the offense against them and move forward with your life.

It's Not a Sign of Weakness

The fear that forgiveness indicates weakness is rooted in the belief that if we don't deal out payback, we open the door for more violations of our boundaries. And yet the truth is, a greater indicator of weakness is allowing the hurtful actions of others to determine your future health and well-being. Stoking your anger may seem like a demonstration of strength, but that's just an illusion. Why not take charge of your own destiny by choosing forgiveness over bondage to anger and fantasies of revenge?

It's Different from Reconciliation

Most of the time, we desire to make peace with those who have harmed us and continue the relationship on better footing. This is called *reconciliation,* a process that can serve to make you stronger and more tolerant of others.

Reconciliation is usually a reasonable course of action unless the damage you've suffered runs deep. If that is the case, then forgiveness is still possible and warranted, for reasons we've already discussed; but it's important to avoid the assumption that forgiveness necessitates reconciliation.

Reconciliation involves evidence of real remorse, restorative measures, and future guarantees of safety. That's a high standard when healing from a serious offense, and it requires the genuine participation of both parties. If it's possible to reconcile with someone who has marred your past, you'll find it to be a source of healing that is in addition to forgiveness.

4 Embrace What Forgiveness *Is*

By understanding what forgiveness *isn't*, I hope you've also gained a better understanding of how forgiveness is an open door to freedom. Now let's explore even more aspects of what forgiveness *is*.

It's a Decision, Not a Feeling

Forgiveness is a rational choice that you make when *you* decide the time is right. It's a determined effort to take authority over past traumas by no longer permitting them to dictate your life. It's liberating yourself from being captive to the past so that you can have a joyful, hope-filled future.

Forgiveness is a strategic, purposeful response to pain and injury—one that can be acted on even if you don't feel like it. The power to forgive is yours, and the ability to forgive can be learned as you choose to take the first step and try.

If you've harbored resentment and a desire for revenge against someone for a long time, your mind will resist your attempts to reverse direction and forgive. To signal that you are serious about getting free, create a contract with yourself. In your journal write,

> I, ____________________, hereby pledge to forgive ____________________ for the following offenses and for the following reasons:

Argue the case on paper for why forgiveness is the right choice. Sign and date it, and then put your journal someplace where you can easily review and recite your pledge when the past threatens to rear its ugly head.

It's a God-Honoring Act

Beyond the personal benefits of forgiveness lies something deeper: By forgiving, you are mirroring the grace God has already offered you. It is your chance to say, "Who am I to make others pay in full for their mistakes when God has forgiven my own?"

Forgiveness is a mental and spiritual posture that invites healing. That's why the Bible so often encourages us with words such as, "Bear with each other and forgive one another if any of you has a grievance against someone. Forgive as the Lord forgave you" (Colossians 3:13). We follow God's example and guidance when we grant forgiveness to others, and in doing so we find peace of heart and mind.

BY FORGIVING, YOU ARE MIRRORING THE GRACE GOD HAS ALREADY OFFERED YOU.

Still, forgiveness does not come easily when someone has inflicted our lives with pain. We must will it, choose it, and learn how to truly *mean* it. Fortunately, the Great Teacher, our gracious heavenly Father, is ready to help us—when we ask.

5 Enjoy the Snowball Effect

Far from being an abstract religious concept, deciding to grant others mercy and grace leads to powerful progress in your journey toward peace. You see, forgiveness is like a snowball rolling downhill: It keeps growing and picking up speed and growing some more.

With the struggling clients I work with, I've seen time and again that learning to forgive lightens their emotional load, brightens their outlook on life, shortens recovery time, and restores their natural resilience against hardships in the future.

YOU ARE YOUR OWN GREATEST ALLY IN YOUR QUESTS TO MAKE PEACE WITH YOUR PAST.

You are your own greatest ally and asset in your quest to make peace with your past. That's because forgiveness is something that can only happen within yourself.

Remember the words of Gina, who chose to forgive her mean-spirited mother: "I just didn't want to live with all that anger and bitterness anymore. The only way to let it go was to forgive."

Those can be your words, too, as you take your own steps toward peace and freedom. In the next chapter, your journey will continue as you travel the path of acceptance.

CHAPTER 3

Travel *the* Path *of* Acceptance

Most people seem to deal with the past by either *denying* it or *dwelling* on it. Neither is a good option for those who want to experience the fullness and richness each day can offer.

Denying a difficult past is like pretending you don't have a broken arm: You may learn to live with the pain, but it won't "set" properly and will, in fact, cause more trouble over the long haul.

Dwelling on the past is like putting a magnifying glass over it, which distorts reality and makes everything seem bigger than it really is.

Try as you might, some things are beyond your control to change. Battling against "what could have been" and "the way it should be" accomplishes nothing.

Spending years bitter that someone betrayed you doesn't undo what happened. Beating yourself up for decades over a youthful mistake can't change the past.

I'm a big believer in acceptance—acceptance of ourselves, acceptance of the wounds we've suffered, and acceptance of the mistakes we've made.

It's important to realize, however, that acceptance is not the same as endorsement: "It's okay that I did what I did."

Nor is it minimizing what happened: "What I went through really isn't that big of a deal."

And it certainly is not blame-shifting: "My parents were terrible role models, so that's why I screwed up."

Instead, acceptance is looking squarely at the situation and acknowledging that what happened, happened. And, yes, there may have been consequences. But that doesn't mean you must relive your mistakes or traumas over and over.

As we seek to move beyond our past, there is no need to either deny it or dwell on it. We can accept failures and hardships for what they are—difficult lessons learned. They are stumbles on the road to acceptance and maturity.

Devin's Story

"I'll never get over it," Devin told me. "My awful mistake will follow me the rest of my life."

The awful mistake he was referring to came to light during a counseling session. Devin had been trying to make peace with his past for years and finally found the courage to entrust his story and emotions to someone who could offer help and perspective.

WE CAN ACCEPT FAILURES AND HARDSHIPS FOR WHAT THEY ARE—DIFFICULT LESSONS LEARNED.

When I asked Devin to share more of his background, he explained, "I had been married to Renae for four years by the time we were both in our late twenties. We'd tried for several years to start a family, and when she finally got pregnant, it seemed like a miracle. But that's when the trouble started for me."

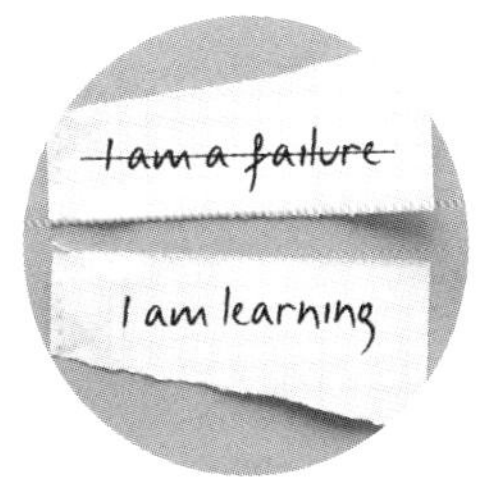

Devin had been raised in a physically and emotionally abusive home by a father who drank too much, raged too much, stormed out too much, and showed way too little love. With significant emotional damage—damage Devin had not worked through—the thought of becoming a father himself caused him to "totally freak out," as he put it.

"One year into being a parent, I just couldn't handle it. I bolted. I left. It was the most cowardly thing I could've done. That was years ago, and I regret it every day. I admit it was the worst thing I could have done to my wife and son. I recognize that I became a version of my own father. Every day is a struggle to know how to live with myself."

When Devin and Renae divorced years ago, they agreed on an arrangement for Devin to stay involved in their son's life. But although he sought forgiveness from his ex-wife and made heroic efforts to become a dad to his son, deep damage had already been done to all involved.

"I failed miserably," Devin told me, "and I've been trying to make things right ever since. Renae says she's forgiven me, but I'm not sure I can ever forgive myself."

Six Principles *of* Acceptance

Perhaps you can relate to Devin's situation. You have your own story to tell about a failure, a poor decision, a pattern of poor decisions, or a disaster you caused.

Finding the strength and wisdom to deal with life episodes—even entire chapters—that we wish we could rewrite is an unavoidable part of the human experience. Every person you meet is on his or her own journey of figuring out how to resolve the tension between the what-ifs and the yes-buts that are inescapable facts of life.

You know that awful mistake you made? It's been made before by others—probably countless times. Or what about that horrible incident you suffered because of someone else's mistake? Other people have also experienced the exact (or similar) hurts or wounds you have.

Dozens of men and women have beaten themselves up in my counseling office. They have said things like "I can't believe I had an affair. How stupid! It wrecked my family," or "I passed up a great job offer because I was afraid I couldn't cut it. Now, six years later, I'm stuck in the same old dead-end job."

You could probably come up with several personal examples—and so could I.

Few people on earth don't have a skeleton or two in their closet—and sometimes enough to fill several closets. Whether these skeletons represent mistakes we've made or hurts we've endured, we're certainly not eager to pull them out and rattle them around in public. Just the thought of sharing them with anyone can evoke feelings of dread and even panic.

FEW PEOPLE ON EARTH DON'T HAVE A SKELETON OR TWO IN THEIR CLOSET.

But reaching out to a safe someone to move that skeleton out of the closet and into the light will accelerate healing. The act of being open and honest—giving words to your experience—will give you the clarity and courage to accept and leave behind the things that weigh you down.

With that in mind, let's take a look at six keys to keep in mind as you travel the path of acceptance—hopefully with the help of someone you trust.

Let these principles encourage and motivate you to keep putting one foot in front of the other.

1 Be Honest with Yourself

When you're in the grip of a past regret or heartache, denial is not your friend, as already mentioned. In fact, it is a huge obstacle blocking a brighter future. When it comes to the past, we must face the truth, the whole truth, and nothing but the truth.

Acknowledging the uncomfortable fact that you messed up or someone betrayed your trust is a first step toward wholeness. Acknowledging that you're still not coping well is also a healthy step.

2 Be Honest with God

As a kid, I learned it was incredibly liberating to own up to something I had done that I wasn't proud of. Trying to hide the deed from my parents, a teacher, or a friend was awkward and exhausting, like walking around with my pockets full of rocks. The moment I told the truth, all that weight disappeared. Even if there were still consequences to face, I learned that confessing my mistakes always made me feel better. Confession set me free from the dread of discovery.

ACKNOWLEDGING THAT YOU'RE NOT COPING WELL IS A HEALTHY STEP.

But there's even more to it. You see, fear of exposure arises, in part, from the deeply embedded sense that we don't measure up to God's standards. While this is certainly true, the fact is that God is not surprised. He knows that we are human. He understands that we need his help to live in a right way, free from guilt. Even if we've done nothing wrong, we may bear the weight of shame or regret over the fact that a traumatic experience has left us filled with anger, rage, or confusion.

The moment we admit our frailties, needs, and fears to God—and ask him for strength, understanding, and forgiveness if needed—we come to the next step: a place where we accept his truth and grace and find the motivation to become the people he created us to be.

3 Embrace Truth and Grace

Perhaps learning to accept the role the past has played in your life is best informed by the words *truth* and *grace*. If we were perfect people with a perfect past, we wouldn't need grace. Truth wouldn't be difficult to accept, for it wouldn't contain the wreckage of our unwise choices or fallout from someone else's poor judgment. In a flawed world, however, grace is a necessity.

I feel extremely blessed to have grown up in a loving, God-honoring family and faith community. Yet as I look back, I realize that the church we attended placed a big emphasis on *doing* rather than *being*. There was plenty of talk about "God's grace" but not much action or attitude to demonstrate what that truly meant.

When I discovered years later that unconditional love is a foundational truth of the Christian faith, I at first struggled to understand what this meant. I'd heard phrases such as "unmerited favor" and "sacrificial love," but I never experienced these realities deep down.

Nobody had clarified this unbelievably good news during my formative years.

As an adult, well into my training to become a psychologist, I came to understand an important truth: Because God created us, our value and worth are established for all time. His love for us is total. There is nothing we can do to make him love us any more or any less.

Understanding that you are freely and completely loved by God will keep your past in proper perspective. You can act on this truth by thinking along these lines: *God loves me, and God wants the best for me. Therefore, I will accept his grace, accept myself, and seek to make the most of the future he has planned for me.*

BECAUSE GOD CREATED US, OUR VALUE AND WORTH ARE ESTABLISHED FOR ALL TIME.

You can tell yourself the truth about where you've been, because the truth of God's gracious forgiveness and his abounding compassion trumps all. You don't need a pain-free, fairy-tale, perfect past to love and accept yourself. And you don't have to wear rose-colored glasses or live in extreme denial to accept what you can't change.

A POTENT HEALING SOURCE

As you work through your hurts and mistakes, equip yourself with the most potent healing source available: the pages of Scripture, from God's mouth to your heart. The Bible testifies of God's love for you—a powerful sustaining force as you make peace with your past:

Nothing can ever separate us from God's love. Neither death nor life, neither angels nor demons, neither our fears for today nor our worries about tomorrow—not even the powers of hell can separate us from God's love. No power in the sky above or in the earth below—indeed, nothing in all creation will ever be able to separate us from the love of God that is revealed in Christ Jesus our Lord.

Romans 8:38-39 NLT

When James and Sharisha came home to a flooded basement, they knew their family of five would need a place to stay until repairs could be made. Thankfully Tye, a coworker of James, invited them to stay at his home. Despite the upheaval in their personal lives, James and Sharisha and their children—ages eight, six, and three—enjoyed the time with Tye and his wife, Tammy, and their three children.

Two weeks later, the basement repairs were complete, so James and his family moved back home. For several days, Sharisha seemed introspective. One night while she and James were getting ready for bed, Sharisha sat down in the chair by the window and turned to her husband.

"Babe, did you notice anything different about Tye and Tammy's house?" she asked.

James looked at her blankly. "Their house? I don't know. Why? You know, the basement game room with the big TV is pretty awesome. Maybe we could do something like that here."

"I'm not talking about the game room," she said. "Did you notice how organized and calm everything seemed? They've got three kids, about the same ages as ours, but somehow Tammy seems to have it all under control—not like me." Her voice sounded on the verge of tears, so James knelt at her side and wrapped her in a hug.

This wasn't a new conversation. Their home *was* disorderly, although not for lack of effort. Even though Sharisha tried to thin out clutter and come up with checklists, issues remained: Almost every room was difficult to navigate. Important items still got misplaced. And sometimes Sharisha forgot to pay bills, racking up fees and debt.

The disarray extended outside of their home too. Sharisha frustrated her children when she dropped the ball on things like paperwork for field trips or class pictures. And while she had a big heart and volunteered for projects at church, she wasn't always able to follow through on the obligations she took on.

Sharisha had *always* struggled like this. As a child, she was often scolded by her parents for her scatteredness, and as a teen, she lost friends because of her flakiness. Sharisha felt more than frustration over this persistent pattern in her life—she felt shame. Some days, her tarnished view of herself seemed to overshadow everything.

When James gently reminded her of all her strengths as a woman, a wife, and a mother, she waved his words away.

"You might see those things in me, James, but I can't see them in myself," she said through tears. "When I look at myself, I see failure after failure."

SHAME VERSUS GUILT

Shame is a strong emotion rooted in the sense that there is something inherently unacceptable about us. It's different from guilt, which is based on behavior ("I *did* something bad"). Shame focuses on your perceived value as a person. Shame incorrectly says "I *am* bad" and has toxic results. But if we acknowledge guilt while rejecting shame, we're on a healthy path toward accepting our potential to blossom into all that God created us to be.

Is there a way to accept unpleasant truths without blaming or shaming ourselves?

A few months after the flooded-basement crisis, James, Sharisha, and their children traveled to spend Thanksgiving with James's sister, Jenny, and her husband, Tom. During their stay, two packages arrived for Jenny.

"WHEN I LOOK AT MYSELF, I SEE FAILURE AFTER FAILURE." —SHARISHA

As Tom brought the packages in from the porch, he said congenially, "Jenny, you have another delivery from the Amazon Fulfillment Center—except obviously your subscription isn't working, because you're never fulfilled! I thought you were going to stop ordering so many things."

Instead of rebuffing Tom for his comment, Jenny replied just as congenially. "You've got a point," she said. "That's four packages this week, right? I think I'll put my online shopping skills on ice for a while."

Sharisha noticed that the brief exchange between Tom and Jenny held no blame or shame from either of them. They had simply observed a pattern they wanted to change, and Jenny responded with a solution.

As the conversation drifted to other topics, Sharisha realized how different their approach was to her own. When *she* spent too much money, her thoughts brimmed with blame and shame: *See, I blew it again. I can't be trusted with a budget. What's wrong with me? When will I ever learn to be an adult?*

Sharisha caught a glimpse, through Tom and Jenny, of truth and grace in action; and as she embraced that simple principle, she began her own journey away from shame and toward self-acceptance.

If shame is keeping you from loving and accepting yourself, don't lose hope. Sharisha found the freedom to become her own biggest cheerleader—and you can too.

Whether on your own or in conversation with a trusted friend or counselor, it's important to draw a line between your value as a person and any painful past experiences or ingrained behaviors that are less than desirable.

Remind yourself that even though you're not perfect, your mistakes don't make you who you are. Likewise, if someone maliciously hurt you, their choice doesn't define you either.

5 State Empowering Truths

One way to overcome shame is to frame an unpleasant truth in a factual and neutral manner. This doesn't mean you are denying the unpleasant truth. It may be true that you cheated on your spouse, you have an addiction to alcohol or food, you were betrayed by someone you loved, or you survived a traumatic childhood—but empowering statements about you are real, too, and God's Word encourages us to focus on the positive truths:

> *Whatever is true, whatever is honorable, whatever is just, whatever is pure, whatever is lovely, whatever is commendable, if there is any excellence, if there is anything worthy of praise, think about these things.*
>
> PHILIPPIANS 4:8 ESV

The following examples illustrate the difference between shame-filled and truthful statements:

SHAME ***A STATEMENT FILLED WITH SELF-BLAME AND EXAGGERATION SAYS . . .***	**TRUTH** ***A FACTUAL AND NEUTRAL STATEMENT SAYS . . .***
"I'm an utter failure at anything that involves money."	"Sometimes I make financial choices that I regret."
"I'm too dumb to do well in school."	"I'm disappointed that I scored 60 out of 100 on the exam."
"I will never succeed at anything."	"When I was growing up, my parents' harsh words led me to think very little of my worth and abilities."

For Sharisha, a powerful and true statement might be, "Even though sometimes my home and life are chaotic, God loves and accepts me. He will never give up on helping me do better."

Stating and believing positive truths about yourself, even if your circumstances or experiences might lead you to believe otherwise, is a potent healing practice.

Here are a few more examples of positive, true statements that can help you make peace with your past. Practice saying each one:

1. "I am more than my mistakes."
2. "I'm capable of learning what I need to learn."
3. "I have value—always."
4. "I am stronger than I think I am."
5. "I can make a difference in the lives of people around me."

Now take one more step. Acknowledge each truth while also acknowledging that because God loves and accepts you, he will help you take positive steps forward.

6 Throw Out Your Timetable

When you're traveling the path of acceptance, there is no magic elixir you can ingest for instantaneous and miraculous relief. The cure will require tough choices, discipline, and commitment on your part. It will take courage to face the emotional dragons you've hidden away in your closet over the years and to dare to think differently about them.

Perhaps most important to understand is that healing the past can't be rushed. There is no one-size-fits-all timetable for recovery. Every situation is unique. True healing takes as long as it needs to take. As psychotherapist Amy Morin notes,

> The well-intentioned adage, "things will get better soon" perpetuates the myth that healing a psychological wound is a passive activity. Unfortunately, waiting to feel better might not yield the best results. Assuming that time heals—and putting a time frame on when you *should* feel better—is dangerous. Not only might you become highly critical of yourself if you don't bounce back fast enough, but you may also lack empathy for other people's prolonged suffering.[7]

The truth is that God is exceedingly patient with us, and he calls us to be patient with ourselves as we persevere in what he's called us to do. Instead of berating yourself for not quickly recovering from past events, take proactive steps to think realistically, regulate your emotions, and act productively. In doing so, you'll build critical resilience on your journey to peace and wellness.

■ ■ ■

As you travel the path of acceptance, take to heart these encouraging words from Scripture: "At just the right time we will reap a harvest of blessing if we don't give up" (Galatians 6:9 NLT). Devin, whom I told you about at the beginning of this chapter, didn't yet understand this concept.

HEALING THE PAST CAN'T BE RUSHED. THERE IS NO ONE-SIZE-FITS-ALL TIMETABLE FOR RECOVERY.

"I'll never get over my past," he said. "My awful mistakes will follow me the rest of my life."

It's true that he will never completely "get over" his mistakes, but he doesn't need to be weighed down by shame and regret for the rest of his life because of them.

If shame and regret are also keeping you from loving and accepting yourself, don't lose hope. Begin today by embracing the insights in this chapter.

Learning to accept yourself and past events that you cannot change allows you to move toward healing as you focus on the things that you *can* change, such as the way you interact with the present moment. This includes eliminating habits that are not serving you well and embracing opportunities that can lead to a better future.

Acceptance doesn't mean living in a Pollyanna world and denying things that are uncomfortable about ourselves or our world.

What it *does* mean is loving ourselves, respecting ourselves, and believing the best about ourselves—even amid imperfection.

When we can do these things, we're in a much better position to enjoy the gift of the present, which we will explore in the next chapter.

THE SERENITY PRAYER

God, grant me the serenity

to accept the things I cannot change,

the courage to change the things I can,

and the wisdom to know the difference.

–Attributed to Reinhold Niebuhr

CHAPTER 4

Make *the* Most *of the* Present

When you travel the path of acceptance, you are no longer paralyzed by the shame or trauma of your past, which also means that you are much better equipped to embrace positive changes that lead to inner healing. That's because the tools you need to heal your wounds and shape your future can only be found in the present. You have the opportunity to take proactive steps that will change the way you view the past and help you interact positively with the present. Let's take a look at four of them.

1 Pay Attention to Self-Talk

We talk to ourselves all day long. It's easy to become so familiar with the sound of our own internal voice that we sometimes don't even recognize it as a voice anymore.

Yet the way that we talk to ourselves matters tremendously. As we saw in the previous chapter, the fact is that our perceptions and statements about ourselves require tending, care, and self-discipline if we are to be free from shame and heal from the past.

THE TOOLS YOU NEED TO SHAPE YOUR FUTURE CAN ONLY BE FOUND IN THE PRESENT.

Make the most of the present by challenging yourself to notice critical, fearful thoughts and to examine their validity. At first, noticing them is enough. There's no need to chide yourself for experiencing them. In fact, doing so may make matters worse.

First, write down any supporting evidence you have for the basis of your thoughts and beliefs. Then write down any evidence that disproves them. After you've looked at both sides, replace those thoughts with statements that more accurately represent the objective truth.

For example, if you were divorced, your thoughts might reflect this belief: *My first marriage ended in disaster, so I'm staying away from romantic relationships. And I certainly would never get remarried—the past would only repeat itself.*

It's true that every dating relationship carries the risk that it might not work out and might even end in hurt. But a highly fulfilling and long-lasting relationship is also a possibility, especially if you have worked hard to learn from past mistakes. In fact, a healthy dating relationship could evolve into a healthy marriage relationship.

To deflate some of the emotional distress that is packed into your beliefs, you could reframe your thoughts this way:

> *Yes, I'm scared about dating again, and that's natural. And I'm afraid of getting remarried because of the painful divorce I went through before. But I recognize that every new dating relationship is a fresh start and a chance to find lasting love, so I will choose to be open to finding a new and healthy mate. I will not be closed to any future possibilities based on my past.*

If you can't talk to yourself kindly, is it fair to expect others to? The way you talk to yourself sets the tone for how you'll engage with the world. Make the most of the present by learning to speak to yourself with more compassion.

AN EXERCISE IN PRESENT-MOMENT AWARENESS

This practice can profoundly reduce anxiety and depression and foster mental and emotional stability. Instead of rehashing the past, your mind becomes trained to stay fixed on the present moment.

Practice this exercise anytime you feel your body tensing up or your mind becoming overwhelmed with repetitive or anxious thoughts. You'll quickly learn what a healing refuge the present moment can be and its powerful effect in making peace with your past.

Phase 1

- Sit in a quiet place where you can remain undisturbed.
- Close your eyes and purposely relax your body.
- Breathe evenly and deeply—cool air in, warm air out.
- Feel the rising and falling of your chest and belly. Focus your mind on these sensations.
- When competing thoughts arise, gently set them aside and return to awareness of your breathing.

Phase 2

- Shift your attention to how your feet feel against the floor.
- Notice the soft pressure of the chair on your legs and back.
- Listen to surrounding sounds—for example, birds singing outside your window or the wind blowing through the trees.

Phase 3

- When you are relaxed and enjoying the pleasure of simply being, expand your mental focus to include everything in the room.
- Ask yourself,
  - *Is there anything present that is frightening or disturbing?*
  - *If I open my eyes, what would I see to remind me of past trauma or regrets?*
  - *Is there any evidence that those issues still pose a threat in my life?*
- The likely answer to these questions is that your fears and anxieties have no actual reason to exist here and now.
- Eventually, these feelings will dissipate when robbed of their connection to reality.

2 Make Healthy Choices

In your effort to cope with the past, it's easy to make unhealthy choices because they are convenient and quick. Indulging in them helps put off the discomfort of facing your past head-on. While drinking too much, isolating yourself, or binge-eating might briefly numb emotional pain, these types of activities will only make the situation worse in the long run.

It's important to make choices that will promote your well-being, not undermine it. When it comes to healing, the end is only justified if the means are safe and healthy. Whatever you're dealing with, give yourself time and space in the present moment to carefully consider your best path forward. There are several ways you can do just that.

Minimize Exposure to Toxic People

If you constantly feel judged for your past and deemed inadequate by workmates, peers at school, friends, or family members, it will be hard for you to believe anything else about yourself. Ending toxic relationships and avoiding contact with difficult people for the time being will help you stay focused on your healing. Granted, there may be some communities from which you can't fully remove yourself at the moment. You might not be in a position right now to change jobs or schools or reduce contact with some family members. Because it's impossible to eliminate *all* toxic people from your life, it's important to surround yourself with those who care about you and appreciate your qualities. This will put you in a much better position to reject the lies of toxic people before they can do damage.

AVOIDING CONTACT WITH TOXIC PEOPLE WILL HELP YOU STAY FOCUSED ON YOUR HEALING.

Limit Social Media

As you commit to healthier choices, make the empowering decision to spend less time on social media. There is often a huge gap between the glamorous online facades people create for themselves and the realities of life. Exposing yourself to this gap every day can foster feelings of inferiority and insecurity. In fact, one study concluded that spending an hour a day on Facebook resulted in a measurable decrease in a person's self-esteem score.[8] Why subject yourself to that? Instead, focus on potent healing sources, including Scripture.

Revamp Your Environment

Making the most of the present includes purging your surroundings of things that tempt you to be less than your best self or that transport you back into a mental space of blame or shame. Relieving yourself of these triggers is a huge step in making peace with your past, so take time to consider how you can care for yourself in this important way.

If you loathe your sugar addiction, rid your home of unhealthy treats. If you feel bad about wasting time on Facebook, remove the app from your phone. If you are drawn into a toxic relationship that decimates your self-esteem, block that contact or change your phone number.

Creating a healthier environment doesn't happen by accident, nor does it happen overnight. But by making it an intentional and consistent priority, you can reap the benefits of treating yourself with nurture and respect.

3 Refrain from Rehashing

Perhaps you can't stop thinking about a past relationship that went sour, or maybe you keep turning over in your mind a traumatic event or a personal failure. There are several strategies you can use to stop or redirect unhelpful thoughts and stay anchored in the present.

Focus on Problem-Solving

First, examine the troubling situation more closely to see if there is anything you can do about it in the present. Of course, many situations that happened in the past are long out of your control, but at least trying to come up with a solution can help you put the situation out of your mind.

TO STAY ANCHORED IN THE PRESENT, STOP OR REDIRECT UNHELPFUL THOUGHTS.

For example, imagine you can't stop thinking about a family relationship that went bad and ended years ago. You keep grieving its loss and your part in the split. These memories weigh on you and cause sleepless nights.

One step you can take is to write a letter to the estranged family member, explaining your perspective and expressing your desire to repair the relationship. Or you could reach out with a phone call or an email. Even if you don't receive a response, you have pursued healing by seeking to intentionally resolve an issue that has nagged at you, and you have sifted and clarified your own feelings in the process.

Distract Your Mind

When you're thinking about something from your past that truly is completely out of your control, your best option might be to distract your mind from thinking about it. Engage in activities you enjoy, which might include:

- Listening to music
- Working on a jigsaw puzzle
- Planting flowers or tending the garden
- Reading a book

Of course, you can't distract your mind forever. But engaging in these practices even for a short time can disrupt the cycle of rumination and bring you back to the present.

Get Moving

Going for a bike ride or a run might be the last thing you feel like doing when you can't stop thinking about the past. But research shows that getting regular physical activity seems to reduce fixating on stressful thoughts to begin with.[9] Even a single session of exercise helps decrease rumination,[10] so if you can't stop thinking about past events that trouble you, consider working out. Any aerobic activity, like power walking, dancing, and swimming, should have the same benefits and can even help decrease anxiety and depression.

THREE SIMPLE WAYS TO SHIFT YOUR THINKING

1. **Write down a specific thought that's been troubling you.** Then try to identify what might have triggered the thought. Did a coworker make a snide remark about a past blunder you made on the job? Did a news report bring up a fear that is related to past trauma? Did a review of your bank statement send you into a panic as you recalled struggles to make ends meet? Once you know the source, you're in a better position to look at it realistically and try to reframe it in positive terms.

Thought:

-

Trigger:

-

2. **On a piece of paper, write down a negative belief that is holding you back.** Now take the piece of paper, fold it up, and throw it in your blazing fireplace or put it through your shredder. As you do, say to yourself, *This belief has been with me for a long time—but not anymore. I am choosing to let it go and replace it with a more positive, more accurate belief about myself.*

3. **Identify several aspects of your life that you feel especially positive about.** One powerful way to shift your thoughts is to *choose* to focus on a positive part of your life, rather than dwelling on what is less than ideal. What do you feel most optimistic about? It might be your work, parenting, marriage, spiritual growth, or creative pursuits. Be as specific as possible, and consider ways you could celebrate how these good things shine brightly in your life.

Positive Aspects of My Life:

-
-
-
-
-

How I Can Celebrate:

-
-
-
-
-

4 Learn to Be Optimistic

Optimism is a key ingredient for every content and successful person. In fact, developing a hopeful, positive, optimistic attitude is far more potent for making the most of the present than many people recognize.

While optimism is its own reward, its benefits extend far beyond a cheery outlook. Studies show that optimism has real, tangible health benefits (again, the mind and body influence one another).[11] But can a person who isn't naturally optimistic develop a sense of optimism? Absolutely. Optimism isn't just something a person is born with; optimism can be learned and exercised, like a muscle.

OPTIMISM IS A KEY INGREDIENT FOR EVERY CONTENT AND SUCCESSFUL PERSON.

Both optimism and pessimism have to do with how we think about our circumstances and the causes of adversity. Take Jack, for example. His car broke down on the way to work. Immediately his mind started swirling with pessimistic views: *If I weren't such an irresponsible person, this wouldn't have happened. I should've been more prepared.*

Jack associated his present dilemma with his past circumstances and believed his entire day would be ruined because of this one setback—an example of faulty thinking and a universally pessimistic view. And since Jack kept chastising himself and blaming his usual bad luck on past experiences, he did indeed have a lousy day.

Now consider Jill, whose car had a flat on the way to work that very same morning. Jill neither wears rose-colored glasses nor blames herself for every little thing that goes wrong. She accepts that sometimes difficult things occur that are beyond her control, and she doesn't allow setbacks to take her mind back to the past or negatively impact how she views herself in the present.

After inspecting her tire, Jill thought, *Well, these things happen. It's no big deal. I'll call a tow truck and catch a ride to work.* Jill accepted the situation, dealt with it, and moved on with her day. Of course, she wasn't thrilled with the hassle and upcoming repair costs, but she kept the predicament in perspective and made a conscious choice to remain positive. Optimism is, at its core, a way of accepting and reframing obstacles. Here are a few strategies for developing your optimism muscle.

Identify Solutions

Brooding over a problem won't change anything. Identifying solutions is empowering and will help you feel self-sufficient and capable the next time a similar problem presents itself.

Practice Gratitude

Each day, make a list of five things you're thankful for—even small things. Soon enough, your mind will naturally focus on reasons to be grateful.

Today I'm thankful for:

1.
2.
3.
4.
5.

Look for Opportunities in Misfortune

Part of what makes a difficult situation so hard to handle is the sense that you are powerless; but that is rarely, if ever, the case. If you suddenly remember something you did or said that offended someone, you now have the opportunity to practice humility and seek forgiveness. If you started a business only to see it fail, you have the chance to examine what went wrong so that it's more likely you'll meet with success next time. The options are truly endless.

■ ■ ■

God's Word encourages us, "Do not be anxious about anything, but in every situation, by prayer and petition, with thanksgiving, present your requests to God." When we do, the promise is that God's peace, "which transcends all understanding," will guard our minds and hearts (Philippians 4:6–7).

THE SENSE THAT YOU ARE POWERLESS IS RARELY, IF EVER, THE CASE.

The mind is one of the greatest assets God gave us to thrive, flourish, and prosper. It can enable us to discover creative innovations, solve difficult problems, and make positive decisions.

Right now, in this moment, you can choose to shape your thoughts and choices in ways that are comforting, reassuring, and life-giving. Are you ready to harness the gift of the present to propel you forward, rather than hold you back? In the next chapter, you'll catch a glimpse of some exciting opportunities the future might hold.

CHAPTER 5

Look Forward *to* *an* Exciting Future

The classic film *Chariots of Fire* tells the story of two British runners: Eric Liddell and his chief opponent, Harold Abrahams. The two men would eventually compete together at the 1924 Summer Olympics in Paris.

Before this, however, Abrahams lost a preliminary race to Liddell and became determined to perfect his technique. Abrahams convinced the famed track coach Sam Mussabini to take him on as a student, and during one of their training sessions, Mussabini showed Abrahams slides of top runners, so he could point out proper form. He focused on a particular image where two runners were at the finish line, with the chest of one pressing through the ribbon.

The second-place runner, a fraction of a second behind, had turned his head to gauge his opponent's progress. This backward glance, Mussabini explained, cost that runner the race. If he had kept his gaze steady and his head forward, the prize would have been his.

Interestingly enough, in the field of counseling, I have met countless people who continued to look backward because of unresolved hurts or regrets from the past. Their momentum was slowed and their progress thwarted because they couldn't forget what happened "back then." The truth is, making peace with your past can't happen until you resist the urge to look back and you resolve to keep your focus on what's ahead.

A great example of this is reflected in the writings of the apostle Paul, who said, "Forgetting what lies behind and straining forward to what lies ahead, I press on toward the goal for the prize of the upward call of God in Christ Jesus" (Philippians 3:13–14 ESV). When we let go of wrongs committed against us and accept ourselves despite the mistakes we made, we are freed from the compulsion to look back. We are liberated from the need to revisit past experiences and replay hurtful episodes.

Another biblical passage picks up on the running imagery: "Let us also lay aside every weight, and sin which clings so closely, and let us run with endurance the race that is set before us" (Hebrews 12:1 ESV). Taking to heart the topics we have discussed—moving from hurting to healing, forgiving others, traveling the path of acceptance, and making the most of the present—enables us to lay aside unnecessary weight so we can run freely and energetically. The race of life is no longer an arduous trudge—it becomes a joyful dash in which our God-given skills and abilities are fully utilized.

God wants everyone to enjoy a life characterized by meaningful relationships, fun adventures, challenging ambitions, and growing character. Let's talk about six steps you can take toward an exciting future flavored with abundance, fulfillment, and contentment.

1 Replenish Your Emotional Energy

For the vast majority of people, life is hectic, stressful, and exhausting. One of our society's most irrational ideas is that we should always push the limits: *Maximize your busyness, speed, and efficiency—then increase it another 10 percent!* While this approach makes us feel productive, it is hard on us mentally, emotionally, spiritually, and physically.

With pressure at work, weekend obligations, household chores, kids and often parents to care for, who has time for rest and renewal? Yet in every area of life, it is crucial to establish reserves—a buffer against the things that deplete you. Here are some tips:

- Allow extra time to complete a project.
- Plan for plenty of time to make it to appointments so you're not constantly hurrying.
- Spend less than you earn.
- Get rid of some possessions rather than acquiring more.
- Try to get extra sleep.

Since all of us are created uniquely, we have different methods for rejuvenating ourselves. For example, extroverts get recharged by spending time with other people. Introverts get recharged by watching a movie or curling up with a good book. Creative people may need to regularly attend the symphony or visit an art gallery. Nature lovers need to go hiking or work in the garden. Identify your boosters and employ them often.

WHEN WE MAKE PEACE WITH OUR PAST, THE RACE OF LIFE BECOMES A JOYFUL DASH.

Keep this in mind, too: Life is full of people, obligations, and tasks that siphon off our energy. Some we can't avoid—but some we can and should. For example, consider cutting back on unnecessary car trips that leave you stuck in traffic, and steer clear of people who soak up your energy like a dry sponge in a puddle of water.

2 Pursue Creativity

Many people find it helpful to process emotions and memories through creative artistic outlets that facilitate healing. Art therapy can be pursued through painting, drawing, dance, drama, music, writing, sculpture, or other forms of self-expression. Over time, these outlets foster self-awareness, self-esteem, improved social skills, and new methods for coping with stress. According to the mental health organization Resources to Recover:

> Studies suggest that art therapy can be very valuable in treating issues such as depression, anxiety, post-traumatic stress disorder and even some phobias. It is a great way to express your emotions without words, process complex feelings and find relief.... Studies also show that creating art stimulates the release of dopamine. This chemical is released when we do something pleasurable, and it basically makes us feel happier. Increased levels of this feel-good neurotransmitter can be very helpful if you are battling anxiety or depression.[12]

Another study found that regardless of participants' artistic ability, forty-five minutes of visual-arts creativity positively affected their mental health and reduced their stress.[13] Additional studies indicate that art therapy can significantly reduce trauma symptoms and depression for people who have had difficult experiences in the past.[14] Caring for yourself by pursuing outlets for self-expression will mark your future with enjoyment and an outlet for coping when difficult aspects of your past might arise.

3 Revive Your Purpose

Many people hear the term *life purpose* and think it applies only to epic, world-changing work. Not so. I define someone's purpose as the *one unique thing* they have to offer the world, no matter how big or small. Its absence might not make headlines, but it absolutely would be missed by those who stand to benefit from a person's one-of-a-kind gift.

Why is finding and following your purpose so important when revitalizing your future? Because purpose is what gets you out of bed on a dreary Monday morning in mid-winter. Purpose is your answer to the question, "Why?"

- *Why keep a grip on my addictive impulses?*
- *Why watch what I eat?*
- *Why care about toxic emotions and their effect on my health and well-being?*
- *Why guard against old habits?*

Your personal purpose may be to pour all your energy into raising healthy children; to teach watercolor painting to residents in a retirement center; to be the most caring and conscientious insurance agent your clients have ever known; or to teach preschoolers in a way that endows them with self-respect and self-confidence. The list of possibilities is infinite. Only you can know which one best describes you.

Because of your unique purpose, you have an important role to play in the lives of others. Those "others" may be everyone who is inspired and moved by a piece of your art, neighbors who are lonely, or church members who are hurting.

The world needs *everyone* to fulfill their purpose—yourself included. This might sound like a cliché these days, but it's never been more true.

To revive your purpose, start by creating a list of things you have loved doing in your life. What you're meant to do now may be something you couldn't stop doing as a younger person but were forced to abandon as you grew older and took on more responsibilities. Or it may be the thing you dare not put on the list but tugs at your heart anyway.

When you have completed the list, take another step by completing the exercise on the next page. Hopefully you will find it helpful in reviving your purpose and dreaming toward your future.

DREAM TOWARD YOUR FUTURE

No matter how difficult your past, I encourage you to dream big and take to heart this promise from Jesus: "What is impossible with man is possible with God" (Luke 18:27). For the next week, spend ten minutes each day thinking about your dreams for the future. Write down your ideas, and then ponder how you might achieve them. Use the following prompts to guide you. This exercise is more than just a feel-good pep talk for yourself; you will be retraining your mind and redirecting your thoughts toward your God-given dreams and purpose.

- Activities I loved to do when I was younger:

____

____

- My reasons for stopping those things:

____

____

- Activities that would make me happy now if money, time, and the approval of others were not obstacles:

____

____

- Possible reasons why I am alive on planet Earth (Hint: Gifts and talents you possess that the world needs):

____

____

- Excuses I've made for not pursuing my dreams and purpose:

____

____

- Steps I can take today to stop sitting on the sidelines and run in the direction of my dreams:

____

____

- Things I can do in the next year to help make my dreams for the future a solid reality:

____

____

Reconnect with Trusted People

We've already discussed how the support and care of other people play an important role in making peace with your past. The same principle applies as you seek to shape a fulfilling future, because relationships are a crucial part of maintaining emotional wellness.

"A FRIEND LOVES AT ALL TIMES."
—PROVERBS 17:17

Numerous studies continue to suggest that social isolation not only robs you of the help others have to give but also invokes serious physical and mental consequences, including an elevated risk of anxiety, depression, and premature death.[15]

Therefore, it's important to determine whether you have enough healthy relational support around you, and if not, to get busy making connections. Seek friendships that are grounded in the following qualities.

Affection

At the heart of all friendships should be genuine affection. Friends enjoy being together because of the way they feel about each other.

Trust

Friends trust each other because each person has proven to be trustworthy. When one friend is tempted to betray the friendship in some way, he or she instead considers the needs and feelings of the other person.

Honesty

One of the hallmarks of true friendship is living within an atmosphere of truth. This truth, however, is not presented in a harsh, brutal manner—but with love, compassion, and tenderness. To a friend, the truth is not a weapon; it is a balm. There is safety in the honest words of a friend, even when those words hurt.

Understanding

True friends know the background and context of each other's lives. They understand the *what* of things, but they also understand the *why* of things. Friends know which way the other will jump and how far, so to speak.

Acceptance

Those who are mature understand the potentially difficult position they put themselves in when they enter into a friendship, because friendship sometimes equates to pain where human beings are concerned. True friends accept the ups and downs of life together as an inevitable consequence of their friendship, and they also understand there is always the potential that one friend could hurt the other.

Sacrifice

There are times when friendship calls for sacrifice. It can be a sacrifice of time, money, energy, resources—a reordering of priorities to put the needs of friendship first. Such sacrifices won't be regretted when balanced against enjoying the rewards of a sustained and lasting friendship.

5 Recover Your Joy

People who have struggled to make peace with their past often forget something important: Life can and should be filled with *fun*. I counsel many people who feel gray and blah with regrets and heartaches. It's like the candy has been stripped out of their lives and only a dry mouthful of cotton is left. Live like that for very long, and the words *pleasure* and *enjoyment* start to sound like they're part of a foreign language.

It's instructive to notice that the word *enjoyment* refers to the process of taking pleasure in something. *Process* and *taking* are active words, things we purposely participate in. We can sit and wait for joy to strike spontaneously, and it sometimes does. But why would we want to wait when it's possible to make it happen by our own initiative? As with so many other things we've discussed, the power of enjoyment is triggered by choice.

If this strikes you as frivolous amid life's serious problems and challenges, remember that God wants us to enjoy abundant lives filled with laughter and rejoicing. Jesus said, "I have come that they may have life, and have it to the full" (John 10:10). It's important that your future includes activities that will replace regret or hurt with joy and contentment. Here are some ways to get the ball rolling.

Step Outside Your Comfort Zone

Start by thinking through specific ways to silence your inner critic, who pronounces judgment on every possible source of fun before you even try it! A rafting

excursion? *Too wet, too dangerous.* A salsa dance class with friends? *Too embarrassing.* A day at the amusement park? *Too childish, too expensive, too loud, too many lines.* The good news is, it's possible to replace objections like these with determined decisions to "just do it." Will this test the boundaries of your comfort zone? Of course. That's what makes it fun!

Make Enjoyment a Daily Habit

Throughout your day, engaging in lighthearted, enjoyable activities will build fond memories and even benefit your health. Studies show that simply getting outside and enjoying nature is good for your brain.[16] What do you like to do: Jog? Bike? Hike in the woods? Go to the gym? Read? Sightsee? You could also consider turning off the news to start a romantic-comedy movie marathon, watch old sitcom episodes, or enjoy performances by clean stand-up comedians.

Have Fun with Friends

Make it your mission to spend time with people who make you laugh and push you to lighten up. Smile so readily that people begin to wonder what you know that they don't. It's up to you: Sit on the shore, or grab a surfboard and enjoy the waves.

6 Renew Your Faith

When well-meaning people advise you to "have faith," they often make it sound simple, as if it's possible to magically "have" something as elusive as faith, on command. That's nearly as unhelpful as telling someone who's suffering from depression to simply "feel better."

Every step on the path to peace requires courage and commitment on your part, and it keeps coming back to one powerful word: *choice*. You must choose to pursue the remedies of a bright future before you can tap into their healing potential. The same is true of faith: to grasp it requires purposeful intent.

True, God is willing and able to meet us exactly where we are and to carry us for as long as it takes to restore our strength. In fact, I believe we would be astonished to see how often we benefit from unseen grace around us.

ENGAGING IN LIGHTHEARTED ACTIVITIES WILL BUILD FOND MEMORIES.

But to actively complete the circuit of God's love, faith is our part to play. Through sheer force of will, if necessary, we do that by choosing to believe we are not alone when the night is at its darkest. God does not need our faith; we do. His strength does not wane; ours does.

Faith, precisely because it begins with a determined choice, is a jolt of energy that activates our spiritual and emotional immune system like nothing else can. How? By opening the door to the one thing that all people lacking inner peace feel they have lost: hope. As the writer of the book of Hebrews assured us, "Faith shows the reality of what we hope for; it is the evidence of things we cannot see" (11:1 NLT).

That writer knew what it meant to hope for something you can't yet see—and he understood that active, determined faith bridges the gap while we wait for what we hope for and believe in to materialize. It means you can *know* you'll have what you seek, because your faith

does not rest in fate or chance or any other thing on earth. Your faith is in God, who is unfailingly good.

WHY NOT ENRICH YOUR FUTURE WITH THE POWER OF FAITH?

One way or another, you always choose how you will face your life: with confidence or with doubt, in strength or in defeat. Given those two options, why not enrich your future with the power of faith? The good news is that with God, you cannot fail—because even if you waver in your faith for a moment, "[God] remains faithful, for he cannot disown himself" (2 Timothy 2:13).

A FINAL WORD

Revise Your Past Narrative

Whether you realize it or not, you tell yourself a story that is related to how you experience every aspect of life. Your narrative consists of your interpretation of past events, current circumstances, and future expectations.

You can't live in the past, and you can't rewrite events from your history. But maintaining a healthy perspective can empower you to revise experiences so that they are less painful and more instructive and so that they honor the person you were and are.

Think about the story you tell yourself *about* yourself. As you look back, do you view your past as a comedy, tragedy, mystery, or adventure?

Your personal narrative matters, because a negative one can keep you stuck in dead-end patterns. If you

A NEGATIVE NARRATIVE CAN KEEP YOU STUCK IN DEAD-END PATTERNS.

tell yourself that a major failure or hurts from the past will forever haunt you, it's likely they will. If you tell yourself that you've never lived up to all you're capable of doing, you probably won't reach your fullest potential in the future.

A negative narrative can serve as a self-fulfilling prophecy. How can you rewrite your narrative and change the script you might be unwittingly living out?

1. Know that your backstory doesn't define you. Good things happen when people stop giving past events the power to hold them back. Audiences cheer when a plucky protagonist stands up and says, "I may not be able to change the past, but I can change my future!" It's a favorite storyline because we know it rings true. The power to stop letting the past define you doesn't just belong to fictional characters or to a handful of lucky people you read about online. That power belongs to you, too, when you live by the truth that "if anyone is in Christ, the new creation has come: The old has gone, the new is here!" (2 Corinthians 5:17).

2. Keep the plot moving forward. Can you imagine a movie opening and ending with a scene where the main character, having given up on life, is sprawled out on the couch watching Netflix and eating a bag of chips—with no action in between? Of course not. Plots are driven forward by intentional decisions and purposeful actions that look toward the future. When the nation of Israel was struggling, God encouraged them with these words: "Forget the former things; do not dwell on the past" (Isaiah 43:18). Don't hesitate to make this true for your narrative as well.

"FORGET THE FORMER THINGS; DO NOT DWELL ON THE PAST."
—ISAIAH 43:18

3. Give yourself a big character arc. A *character arc* refers to the inner journey of a character over the course of a story. The best stories involve characters who grow into better versions of themselves as a result of their circumstances. Be that kind of character in your own story. James 1:3–4 says, "The testing of your faith produces perseverance. Let perseverance finish its work so that you may be mature and complete."

4. Enlist the help of a script doctor. Experts are often hired to rewrite or polish existing scripts. Don't hesitate to enlist the help of a professional if you're having trouble rewriting your narrative on your own. Partnering for a season with a counselor or trusted mentor may be just what you need to begin seeing your story in a whole new light.

Now take some time to identify one experience you consider painful or cringe-worthy, and consider how you can revise it to draw out important lessons and positive outcomes that will serve you now and in the future.

- Ideas for revising my narrative:

  ____

  ____

  ____

  ____

  ____

  ____

  ____

  ____

  ____

Notes

1 Quotations from Mo Isom are taken from "Mo Isom, Former LSU Goalkeeper and NY Times Bestselling Author," *Sports Spectrum Podcast,* April 21, 2017, *Sports Spectrum: https://sportsspectrum.com/podcast/2017/04/21/new-podcast-former-lsu-goalkeeper-ny-times-bestselling-author-mo-isom/*, as well as from *Wreck My Life: Journeying from Broken to Bold* (Baker Books, 2016), where Mo shares her full story.

2 Mark D. Seery, E. Alison Holman, and Roxane Cohen Silver, "Whatever Does Not Kill Us: Cumulative Lifetime Adversity, Vulnerability, and Resilience," *Journal of Personality and Social Psychology* 99, no. 6 (2010): 1025, *https://escholarship.org/content/qt4b6787gk/qt4b6787gk.pdf.*

3 Georgia Witkin, "The Power of Talking: Why Experts Advise to Talk about Your Feelings," August 9, 2018, *Psychology Today: https://www.psychologytoday.com/us/blog/the-chronicles-of-infertility/201808/the-power-of-talking.*

4 Steven C. Hayes, "Four Fs That Make a Difference: How to Build True Commitment beyond Mere Faith in Yourself," November 8, 2022, *Psychology Today: https://www.psychologytoday.com/us/blog/get-out-your-mind/202211/four-fs-make-difference.*

5 "Forgiveness: Your Health Depends on It," accessed March 26, 2025, *Johns Hopkins Medicine: https://www.hopkinsmedicine.org/health/wellness-and-prevention/forgiveness-your-health-depends-on-it.*

6 Mayo Clinic, "Forgiveness: Letting Go of Grudges and Bitterness," November 22, 2022, *Mayo Clinic: https://www.mayoclinic.org/healthy-lifestyle/adult-health/in-depth/forgiveness/art-20047692.*

7 Amy Morin, "Study: Time Won't Heal Your Psychological Wounds," March 20, 2016, *Forbes: https://www.forbes.com/sites/amymorin/2016/03/20/study-time-wont-heal-your-psychological-wounds/?sh=3e9219cc6dec.*

8 Muqaddas Jan, Sanobia Anwar Soomro, and Nawaz Ahmad, "Impact of Social Media on Self-Esteem," *European Scientific Journal* 13, no. 23 (August 2017): 329–41, *https://www.researchgate.net/publication/319396436_Impact_of_Social_Media_on_Self-Esteem.*

9 Eli Puterman, et al., "Physical Activity Moderates Stressor-Induced Rumination on Cortisol Reactivity," *Psychosomatic Medicine* 73, no. 7 (2011): 604–11, *National Library of Medicine: https://www.ncbi.nlm.nih.gov/pmc/articles/PMC3167008/.*

10 Serge Brand, et al., "Acute Bouts of Exercising Improved Mood, Rumination and Social Interaction in Inpatients with Mental Disorders," *Frontiers in Psychology* 9 (March 13, 2018): *https://www.frontiersin.org/articles/10.3389/fpsyg.2018.00249/full.*

11 Eric S. Kim, et al., "Optimism and Cause-Specific Mortality: A Prospective Cohort Study," *American Journal of Epidemiology* 185, no. 1 (January 1, 2017): 21–29, *Oxford Academic: https://academic.oup.com/aje/article/185/1/21/2631298.*

12 Mary Ann Cohen, "Creativity and Recovery: The Mental Health Benefits of Art Therapy," July 10, 2018, *Resources to Recover (rtor.org): https://www.rtor.org/2018/07/10/benefits-of-art-therapy/.*

13 Girija Kaimal, Kendra Ray, and Juan Muniz, "Reduction of Cortisol Levels and Participants' Responses Following Art Making," *Journal of the American Art Therapy Association* 33, no. 2 (May 23, 2016): 74–80, *National Library of Medicine: https://pmc.ncbi.nlm.nih.gov/articles/PMC5004743/.*

14 Dafna Regev and Liat Cohen-Yatziv, "Effectiveness of Art Therapy with Adult Clients in 2018—What Progress Has Been Made?" *Frontiers in Psychology* 9 (August 29, 2018), *https://www.frontiersin.org/articles/10.3389/fpsyg.2018.01531/full.*

15 Amy Novotney, "The Risks of Social Isolation," *Monitor on Psychology* 50, no. 5 (May 2019): 32, *American Psychological Association: https://www.apa.org/monitor/2019/05/ce-corner-isolation.*

16 Chris Mooney, "New Research Suggests Nature Walks Are Good for Your Brain," June 29, 2015, *The Washington Post: https://www.washingtonpost.com/news/energy-environment/wp/2015/06/29/fixating-or-brooding-on-things-take-a-walk-in-the-woods-for-real/.*

MORE RESOURCES FROM DR. GREGORY L. JANTZ

Unmasking Emotional Abuse

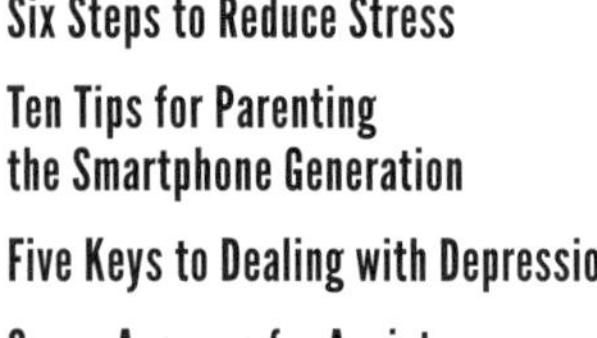

Six Steps to Reduce Stress

Ten Tips for Parenting the Smartphone Generation

Five Keys to Dealing with Depression

Seven Answers for Anxiety

Five Keys to Raising Boys

Freedom from Shame

Five Keys to Health and Healing

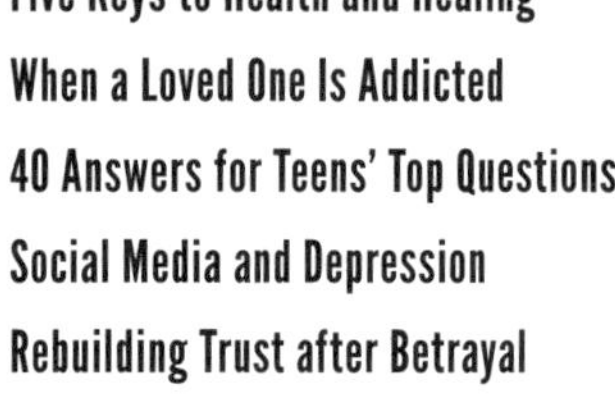

When a Loved One Is Addicted

40 Answers for Teens' Top Questions

Social Media and Depression

Rebuilding Trust after Betrayal

How to Deal with Toxic People

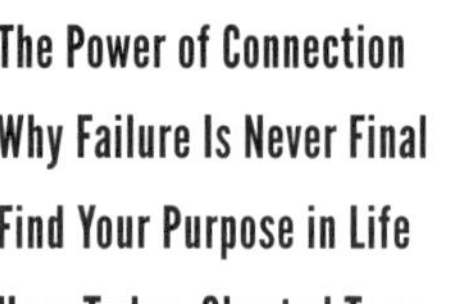

The Power of Connection

Why Failure Is Never Final

Find Your Purpose in Life

Here Today, Ghosted Tomorrow

Beyond Burnout

Make Peace with Your Past

Healing After Loss